Once Houses Could Fly

Once Houses Could Fly

KAYAKING NORTH OF 79 DEGREES

Rosemary Clewes

George Payerle, Editor

Signature
EDITIONS

© 2012, Rosemary Clewes

All rights reserved. No part of this book may be reproduced, for any reason, by any means, without the permission of the publisher.

Cover design by Doowah Design.
Photo of Rosemary Clewes by Paddy Duncan.

This book was printed on Ancient Forest Friendly paper.
Printed and bound in Canada by Hignell Book Printing.

We acknowledge the support of The Canada Council for the Arts and the Manitoba Arts Council for our publishing program.

Library and Archives Canada Cataloguing in Publication

Clewes, Rosemary, 1935-
    Once Houses could fly / Rosemary Clewes.

Poems.
ISBN 978-1-897109-93-9

    I. Title.

PS8605.L543O53 2012   C811'.6   C2012-901745-0

Signature Editions
P.O. Box 206, RPO Corydon, Winnipeg, Manitoba, R3M 3S7
www.signature-editions.com

in memory of
Irene M. Carrick
(Auntie Rene)
1889-1977

CONTENTS

13 ... PREFACE

15 ... THREE POEMS

21 ... STILLNESS HAS AN ECHO

31 ... ELLESMERE ISLAND FACT SHEET

37 ... HOW BIG IS THE WORLD?

51 ... I HAVE WORSHIPPED LIGHT

71 ... EVERYTHING WAITS TO BE SEEN

89 ... THE WORLD MADE WHOLE

103 ... NOTES

107 ... ACKNOWLEDGEMENTS

109 ... ABOUT THE AUTHOR

I had wanted to suckle the light
the land to mirror my desires
and the daily bread of beauty
given to please my eye

I had wanted to take my grief in small bites

yet it is on record that the Twin Glaciers
at Alexandra Fjord are uncoupled now
and walking inland; cycles
once linked are breaking.
I stand on the threshold
of wind born calamity
ice-lock caving to rain,
high tech toxins in Inuit milk.
Not only the birds see
how maps are redrawing whitest habitat
in brown and blue.

—Rosemary Clewes
2010

PREFACE

We travelled as a group of ten, to the Kane Basin on Ellesmere Island in August of 2004. I had heard rumours about *weather and a hard trip* on the Canadian side of Smith Sound, and having kayaked on the more dazzling northwest coast of Greenland in 2002, I was uneasy. I wanted to hug that first kayaking experience of light and ice, imagining foolishly that it could somehow be diminished. I feared I was not ready for whatever Ellesmere Island had up its sleeve.

But for all that, I was eager for the roofless world and its whispered voices, which are always present if you know to listen for them. We left Ottawa for the Arctic's east hub, at Resolute Bay, then the following day took a three-hour flight in our chartered Twin Otter to put down at our destination on the deserted shores of Alexandra Fjord.

One thing that's different about Ellesmere Island is the absence of people. We did not see any Inuit hunting, or signs of summer camps as we had in Greenland. Thus our unwitnessed passage fed my sense of a world from which living history had fled. Strangely, because of this, I wanted to find my place here, to seek a closeness to the land I had not experienced before.

Early on in those twelve days of kayaking in the High Arctic, I gave up longing for the sun to illuminate our voyage and drive away the cold. From Baffin Island to the south, a weak weather system tracked us with stacked cloud-cover, lashing rain and wind. It was heady stuff, that wind.

Believe me, I could count the hours of sunshine for the whole trip on one hand. That lack, transforming the stark simplicity of landforms into a monochrome stronghold of primitive power, frightened me. Deprived of my delight in shadow's vocabulary, I found my acceptance of what was given sorely tested.

In the beginning we paddled inside *...the sweep / of the sky and sleeping ocean—/ light's unpearling mantra lov(ing) us from afar...*, but this dogged front forced my hand. *Wait and see* became the mantra of our days, as a floating barrier of ice at the mouth of the fjord threatened to block our route in any direction. I should already have known how this polar desert dismantles expectations.

Many days we were land-bound. But it was when we paddled a long distance on a cold night that the coastal rock's desolate monotony broke open my heart. My *crie de coeur* ran like this: *There must be something behind beauty.* Not this dark emptiness. Yet, was this not what I had come for? The fierce unknown. The estrangement. The mountain's unadorned face.

I could not bear to write about this for two years. I lived with sorrow, and feeling the weight of it at my back I allowed it to simmer, almost out of sight, yet not completely. When a man named Eric asked me if I loved all creation, I knew I did not. This book recalls the journey as a summoning to myself: a humility, which does not anticipate my competence, which opens its arms to the unfolding world.

THREE POEMS

Can you find Ellesmere Island on your globe?

                                                     That one,
six decades ago, revolved in its mahogany cradle—
when I was barely tall enough to tilt the north pole with a finger
I traced the convolutions of coastline: archipelago's strew

Whole continents foreshorten reaching for the poles
Canada's bulk spreads like a hand stretched wide
                                                            big-hipped at the 49th
I cup her coolness in my palm, hold or spin the world at will
                                                                         Colours fly

The gentle art of mapmaking
shades Arctic reaches, green and white;
                            orange for Argentina, Chile;
yellow for Russian steppes

Whoever coloured these worlds charted ownership
                                                       boundaries as bounty
Imperial Britain's great scatter forever pink

                                     At ten, I memorized every sea
then took to rivers   "Yangtze" has a fine ring
I thought maps spoke a singular truth   Once drawn
how could they change?
                                   Round earth projected on flat paper
gave us the globe at a glance,
until Apollo 8 showed us a small blue
heaven, earth's loveliness fixed in our minds forever

                              Dissatisfaction
gnaws now, as forests dwindle
I want to shake off the colours laid over the wild—
fathom Beaufort, Tatshenshini, Ellesmere, Inglefield Fjord
where last year's ice-towers altered passage around islands—
growlers, once sealed to rock, nose-dive into ocean
as ice re-charts itself

I know what it's like to walk the inner map
where printed names on shorelines do not bristle
                    Listen now
for the avalanche's thunder
summer meltwater's urgent voice   for the great change
sweeping our cold strongholds of the North

                         The night
before I go to the High Arctic
I dream

          dawn's leaf-dark streets lose
the city
of the Old One's hidden face
wise in the way of the silent world

My primitive brain remembers
                         escape by falling
a one-way bridge   river rising under   Once
it was easy to jump
                innocence
unarmed   or me just sleepwalking —

but she's a deep one
delivers me from animal fear   river flood
rebel ice scuttling kayaks

                    I am one of the hunted ones —
why?   six times the river rises   six
times falls   six gilded water-waders rescue me
from runaway ice
                unlock the river's sluice
Ready or not
            I jump

The river gets higher every time I come

Wilderness does not endorse us as humans, it includes us as mammals.

—Don McKay

STILLNESS HAS AN ECHO

Weather always iffy over the polar desert,
but signs good for flying to Ellesmere Island
this morning. Clear sky, no rain or fog-hover.

>Eager now to move out.
>Pilot and co-pilot flying by hand, head and instinct
>rocket us into high summer adventure

that could change us forever—

besides, I had to come. Some great wind bearing me north.

What stories are told by this place
beyond the primal arrangements,
the wilderness of cold?
This harsh order
where no living dust excites the heart.
The shore gives way to alluvial plains,
silver tributaries and rivers born of summer.
Over Jones Sound and Makinson's Inlet
the wind-scraped peaks
belly up mammalian shapes breaching
out of bedrock,
framed by snow.
Scarfed and lost in myself,
we fly the miles over the Arctic Cordillera.
The light is sudden and lovely,

and I'm grateful
for unbroken silence below the plane's drone
for space that never lets up
for the unsullied earth
for wind's whip over polar desert
for time, out

>   out past the red engine, its prop's blur,
>   a blue fjord licks the granite cliff
>   where ice sails in the sun.

Over the abandoned runway at Alexandra Fjord,
we sweep low,
check for boulders, bears, ditches,
then veer hard — above one wing
                                            remorseless earth
bevels up, ready to assassinate,
but we level
                bounce
                        brake within yards.
Settle.
        The pilot kills the switch.

                    My back is half turned
when the Twin Otter lifts and circles, its buzz
cut like an umbilical cord by the mountain's head—
but we're not away—not yet—
an outhouse, roothouse, clapboard buildings
scattered here comprise a Science Station.
Botanists use the outhouse. I do too
until I learn they don't like it.

They don't speak to us when they see us.
Adding shit to the honey bucket means cleaning
twice in a season. Understood.
Of course, north of 80 degrees you tend to notice strangers.
Heck! The creek is only three city blocks away.

        Five kayaks lined up on the beach—
by every hatch, a mountain of gear
Looks impossible   laughable even
                              but we stow it.
Scott and I, paired (from leader's bow
uninterrupted view, a bonus). Denise and Dale take sterns
ballast for lightweight Luciano Napolitano and Brand.

I kneel by the empty hatch, fist-firm tent poles into tapered bow
punch three colour-coded stuff-sacks, padding curves—boots,
toe-first
and right-side-up— coax a jar of antipasto into one heel.

Geologist Gerry paces stern to bow, calculating logistics—
Wife Cookie, arms akimbo, just waits.
This from a guy who's done it all before.
    Doesn't he know their sacks
are the size of seal bladders?
    I'll believe it when I see it!

That Dale. Stuffing hunter's gear—
    1940s duck tents come to mind.
In jeans, he'll freeze but won't listen
    to Scott's Arctic expertise,
his orange toque a cinder in the Arctic's eye.

Hand it to the honeymooners,
Marty teaching lawyer Chris,
so quietly, all done
            Watching us.

I top the hatch with wine in wobbly silver skins,
stretch neoprene cover, seal the rim. Brand winks,
thumbs up. Packed small, I buckle the lid.
Food divided, eggs stowed safely on the deck.
Where's the lunch? will echo more than once.

Ready or not, we set forth in the evening.

Skraeling Island lies out there
calm and cold.
                     For a heady moment I fancy
I am born to paddle—
                            but wary suddenly
                                     in the harbourless world
where shifting reflections and the story of Sedna
conflate in my mind.
                    Just there
bobbing around my kayak
         the bloody joints of tiny fingers—
her screams and the furious father cutting her
loose from the gunwale to sink. He sold her
to a dog for his own survival
                            and like a wrecked ship
she took revenge to the bottom of the sea.
                       There, the animals were birthed
from those uncoupled fingers
                         which she released
through the forest of her tangled mane.

Sedna, Spirit of the Sea, listen—
I honour you   your undersea abode
lies beneath my bow   Mother of mammals
I promise to leave no footprint for you to punish
O powerful undine   send up
the whiskered ones for air—
let me rewrite your tale as faithful Cordelia
let me amend your heart

—but I am drifting into enchantment
during safety drill,
                    Walrus are tricky Scott warns—
like to pick off a stray   Raft up to rescue
lend one end of your paddle to another
for a second pair of hands
Work fast if man overboard
haul your mate onto the makeshift deck
strip off the wet and dress in dry

We never listen to in-flight spiels
but we pay attention to this

ELLESMERE ISLAND FACT SHEET

Ellesmere Island: the northernmost island of the Arctic Archipelago. Canada's third-largest island.

Co-ordinates 79.874297 N° — 79.321289 E°

Ellesmere lies 2,500 miles from the nearest highway
    2000 miles from the nearest tree
    600 miles from the North Pole
    is 500 miles long and 82,119 square miles overall.

Named by British admiral Edward A. Inglefield after Frances Egerton, 1ˢᵗ Earl of Ellesmere, in 1852.

Kane Basin named after Elisha Kane, whose expedition in search of the Franklin Expedition crossed it in 1854.

In the shape of a giant seastack, Ellesmere is covered with glaciers and ice. Barbeau Peak, the highest mountain peak in Nunavut (2616 m), is located in the British Empire Range.

There are four Polar Oases, or areas of local warmth, on Ellesmere:
    Eureka,
    Lake Hazen,
    Tanquary Fjord and
    Alexandra Fjord.

Typical day for us, 40° F.

Ellesmere's population in 2001: 168 over three settlements.

Alert, the northernmost settlement in the world. In winter, 50 people with the Canadian Forces Station (CFS).

Eureka. A handful man the "airport" at "Fort Eureka," which houses the quarters for military personnel, the Environment Canada Weather Station and the Polar Environmental Atmospheric Research Laboratory (PEARL).

Grisle Fjord on the island's south shore, 100 people.

Ice News:
Summer 2002, The Ward Hunt Ice Shelf, off Ellesmere Island's northwest coast, broke up.

In 2005, the Ayles Ice Shelf cracked, sending the "Alyes Ice Island," some 66 square miles in all, on a three-year journey through the Arctic Archipelago.

In 2008, The Serson Ice Shelf lost 60 percent of its total area, and the 4,500-year-old Markham Ice Shelf broke away from Ellesmere Island and floated into the Arctic Ocean.

We need to witness our own limits transgressed.
—Henry David Thoreau

HOW BIG IS THE WORLD?

From kayak to shore-ice
I need tusks
ice-axes
to haul out at sea-edge
landing's slick slope
an underwater jetty

From now we'll be sniffing the wind
index held to the lead-legged sky
hunting (praying) for sun signs

what will be given
beyond the gods' icy whims

Vacant campsites always feel lonely

                          We come   then vanish
                          They come   then vanish
                                       centuries

The crouching hills' long practice of silence

                          Should I ask for hospitality—bow first?

Morning is a mum mirror
'til I unzip silence
crackle underboot like BB shot
tears up space

                                        No one shape to fix my eye
                                        no "keer-keer" of the arctic tern
                                        kicking up heels inside clouds—

ice cubes   big as rooms
                        list
                               in water's black abyss

Skraeling's earth was inscrutable 'til the dig in 1977—
Schledermann's trowel   rearranging tundra's legible face

qammaqs   Thule houses   Stone slabs of walls caved over
charred hearthstones   half-buried & grassed up

Spines-shins-shoulders   plentiful proof of walrus   whales
A bowhead's backbone contrives an anklet for a god

then a bloom in the mind   brittle lichen of abundant death
so whimsical in the unrelenting cold

They lead me to the undeniable   to the end
where there is no end
to pattern   this upwinding
of nature's boneyard   heeled in
then turfed out

Primal words were spoken here
                              by snow hare and fox
                              bringing light to the world.
First babies picked out of earth like flowers
filled the pockets of purple mountains
dropping pleated skirts from the sky.
                              Once houses could fly.

First questions were born
                How big is the world?
That's what I want to know   what I came for—
to travel where the world meets itself beyond fiction
where what is said to be so   is so.
                              The truth of bleached bones
wind-seared skeletons—I came for rock
that dependable middleman between sky and ocean
binding worlds.
                Each world
holding to its own place.

I go here because the land   so sparsely peopled
is hard to plunder.

Just as nobody owns the seal in the sea
  Nobody has a right to possess a house

Try reconstructing, from subterranean traces, a stone-age race. Sit them up, dress them like dolls that do not feel the cold like me, my skinny cheeks, unsuitable nose, bones cold just thinking. Comfort's plenty draws a blank. We never talk of lice, shit, where to shoot the snot, seal oil's black stench, sweat, love's hands, the killing survival depends on.

TAKES 50 SEALS A YEAR TO FEED A FAMILY—

Ugjuk   great seal hunted in middle depths
         carcass divides by seven   Food, boot-soles, ropes

Nattiq   ring seal for hunting bladders, boots, clothing, rugs, oil, meat

Aiviq   walrus for blubber, meat

Qilalugaq tuugaalik   narwhal for *maktaaq*, fuel, tusk and
                       bone house supports

Qilalugaq qaulluqtaq   beluga for meat, blubber and *maktaaq*

Tiriganiaq   fox, for clothing, meat when starving

Nanuq   polar bear, meat   One bear, two pair pants

Today we hunt for garnets
scratching glassy eyes out of the flaky schist with fingers.
I can't help the loneliness I feel.
Sometimes I keep my head down so that I can measure what I see.
Naming is like ownership of the heart,
like finding new love. Now I look everywhere for garnet-ruby rivers
streaking the metamorphic clays and micas.
Here, in God's workshop,
His orderly household strips me human.

> Time for the arctic loon means
> countdown to migration.
> It glides into the pool's tranquility,
> stuffs a fish into the open-shut-chutes
> of the ever ravenous chicks
> then rises again.
> Inside, its little ticker is
> a heart for its family,
> circling the tundra pond.

Plankton feeds krill, feeds whales—
decapods, amphipods and cod, seals.
What's hardest to see
is felt as presence—
raw materials forming the river in us all.

                    Rules are
we pack a plastic plate,
mug, bowl and cutlery — mine
stored briny in a blue net bag —
not lavish like the crested silverware strapped to sleds
the Franklin survivors harnessed
to their bodies
                    for the fatal trek south —
nothing too fragile or clumsy
to cumber the strict permission
prescribing only a book, a small story perhaps,
to displace the wild outside the tent,
the infinite, as it creeps its sudden weather
into our dreams, rattling sleep.

I loved Luciano's box of matching dishes,
printed with runaway flowers,
escaped, no doubt, from the Villa Borghese Gardens
in Rome. How he imagined solace here,
and after eating, soaked them clean
in the pale salt sea.
Stowed them then, under the pretty lid.

I saw Scott's heel wield the authority
his mouth chose not to utter,
swift and implacable to flatten the box
too big to plant between his feet while paddling.

When Scott returns the dishes to his hands,
Luciano's face.

We island-hop east from Skraeling to Alexandra Fjord looking for walrus.

Our kayaks hardly cause a wrinkle on the surface

Let's say this priceless light under Riphean skies
is like Versailles without the gold
that the ice is multi-year ice
and no longer as young and innocent as the frozen pond
where I skated on my double runners when I was three

Take mirror, mirage and yes, maybe replica
mindlessly multiplied,
tip over all the hill-cliffs' looming forms
then lay them down in liquid silver.
Add ripples, red kayaks and tiny licks and laps
then hold this mirror high, just above your ear
and listen, now, to the grief of strange mutations
Edgar's lament,   *Life would not yield to age*

No terra firma here
on this becalmed accumulation of floes
but buoyed, always buoyed
by the turquoise tulle of their sub-aqua tutus
Primed with laughter and for the umpteenth time
the ice conducts its ancient airs and dances for the light
                                                          But wait—
the walrus' walloping breath, heads like wet rocks
                                                      entering the mirror

Nothing breaks the sweep
of sky and sleeping ocean —
light's unpurling mantra loves us from afar,
tilts uncertain gods in my face
                I feel my eyes could penetrate like spears
the deep drifting beneath our lazy red kayaks —
invisible currents carve the violet undersong of ice

As if the universe unstopped its lungs
                      to suck air out of clouds
the sea opens like a lisp
and walrus advance
                between tremendous breaths
my own lungs suddenly bereft
                They arc and dive in twos and fives
braiding   somersault in spirals — gregarious
Vikings in shiny helmets chasing two-pronged tails
unravelling the speechless water
watching us with mean ruby eyes

Should I mark more than shining hours?
—Evan S. Connell, Jr.

I HAVE WORSHIPPED LIGHT

Don't know why, there's no sun up in the sky, stormy weather…

Sky opens, slams shut. Thin cloud, hovering above the fjord, splits the distance between the mountains and me. Southeast, in open sea, the ice pack walls up the horizon. (If only the wind would blow it away, we could paddle to Pim Island.) Twenty-five miles northeast, toward the Bache Peninsula, silver rain slants through storm-decked clouds—weather, more complex than all Arctic history put together, is only one factor testing our forecaster skills.

Another is the current: the way it eddies, invisible almost, pushing ice around (as smooth as horizontal escalators along airport-levels, gliding bodies through space) until, that is, the ice is on top of ME, an hallucination from memory…

> *I grab the emergency oar from the floor of the Zodiac and thrust the paddle end toward the woman in the one beside me. "Swing our bow out,"*
>
> *I shout. She pulls hard and we come free. Tall ice, riding the current, is bearing down on us: closing in. Wedged: three Zodiacs pinched from three sides; rubber screeching and the inside one trapped and tipping. Passengers standing, crouching, trying for the best camera angle to capture a polar bear and cubs sleeping 200 yards away on an ice floe begin to panic. These damn sailors driving the boats, gawking too.*

These seconds frozen in my mind, yet—
in mid-cry, mesmeric
the current's brimming, glassy swill
its jaws

Ice funnels in   out of fjords
a tidal dither mapping new shorelines
in six-hour shifts
Days and dates stall
old habits flip belly-up

Though not hunting for food
we're living closer to the Inuit way

Is this breakfast, Cookie?
Don't know—first meal of the day,
should be the second
or maybe we just skipped that—
it's afternoon and we haven't had lunch

Meals under tarp, rain pissing on-off.
I'm ornery, mean-minded.
Yet — there's power
in the unshakeable light
in just sitting
waiting it out
when you can't run
turn it off   on
nothing to do   alone together —
better than kicking ass.

There is only one arctic tern
black cap & pale wings   unmistakable
   If you're thinking gull
                Ross   Ivory   Sabine   Glaucous
   look for her forked tail

        She's livid we're camping here
           our to'ing and fro'ing too near the nest—
chicks she's feeding up
        for summering in Antarctica—
Her yellow eye pegs me climbing
between the outcrop and sea-side cliff
                She spins
her skywheel   fishing for me
        Holy Smoke!
Did you see how she back-pedals
            attacks?
Run   run   run
        arctic tern
misses the tail on the donkey by the width of a hair

We departed for a new camp in Buchanan Bay.

Paddling late, the bilateral dip of my blade strict
as a pendulum with no hand to stop it.
I am Time's mute partner,
slipping under the loom of shore's mud-brown walls.
I cannot say precisely where
our new camp lies
or how we will know it —
somewhere inside *civil twilight*,
under a midnight sun gone 6 degrees south,
or worse —
         sky heeling in
the last breath of light.

Dare I wish for a map's overview
where what's what is laminated blue,
and names, the likes of Kane, Bache and Buchanan
erase anonymity?

Predictably, I fiddle the odds.
Now I am pagan, monist, or by turns, mystically impulsive.
I beg a tangible divinity, a hymn to sing.
Suffer me trance, I cry, that I might swim through rock.
I would take any epiphany looking for home —
but please, please don't lose me.

If this planet still smolders in its heartless behold
send me a live coal — bring me
a chariot of fire, a bow of burning gold.
Is this rock-womb Sedna's bad joke?
What gods' brute feet tread on the mountains here?

Yet, yet, my spine survives and my eyes are open.
Is this twisted cordillera not the Golden City's ramparts?
Ellesmere's dirty smudge under steely sky, my home tonight?
I say, fear the granite shore swaggering like thunder,
its courage to step into sky,
                        but I must believe in something.

                  Tonight I am a tired witness.
My mind unable to leave bone for ether —
but quickly,
        pecking there
                between shore-fast erratics
                          the Ruddy Turnstones
flashing wing-white wings, sparkle
under the oblivious sky.

We paddle too far
                retrace the miles.
Seeing how sight deceives
river music would be one thing I'd listen for,
its unquenchable song.

This wilderness of stone and deep time
inhabits the world like a cold force—
the land
       a first casting   a rough maquette
  lumbering
           into new form
on God's own timetable.
                         God as a rock?

Do life forms appear as an afterthought in the mind of rock?

Seen from afar
tundra's weft is unreadable —
  its dog-eared valleys
conceal a garden rumoured to be underfoot

  and where cottongrass leans east
                            this plateau
flat as a continental plate
                still flaunts the calamity of drift

What you can't see is
a mountain-fed marsh in the slant light

Three million years ago
  this slow waltz of rafted rock
                     straddled the equator
Fins became limbs
  when *Tiktaalik Roseae* slid shoulders
onto land out of anoxic water   gulping warm air
among the ferns and horsetail
                  The birth of trees
What was
       is
           our Devonian bridge
                      to upright

Up close at Buchanan Bay
seed capsules atop tall stalks court wind.
Red moss like smoke fans across
the valley floor, autumn's window
wide open on the apricot and leather
leaves of blueberry, the honeyed grasses
skeltered in between.

Midline and low a melt river flows
everywhere the trickle and glitter
of the tea-brown bog. I had to tread
on the hummocks' gardens
closing my ears to the crunch of wiry stalks—
boot bruise unavoidable.
The ooze and suck a rude rhythm
making music of the end of summer.

                After rain
all half-dark polar night
and a waiting-on-weather kind of day
I wander down to the pond's edge
scoop handfuls of ice water over my face
                        sit back on my heels
alone
then unarmed, shaken
by light that comes from beyond itself—
the way it dumps distance into my lap
Every compass point a freedom
                      I could go in any direction
only the seabirds would know
they don't give a hoot
for solitude's sweet ache or me

Do I encroach on souls reciting their thin names
birds incanting to bone what must be told again?

                          How well I know my part—
a good tripper they say, stem strong long after the petal's release,
muscle-speak now playing me up like a puppet.
Am I wind's ventriloquist? "Dog tired," it croaks.

The sky, suddenly too wide flung—cloud wrung—awe used up.
I'm not wasting an opportunity to talk to God if I crawl
into the sack and doze.

Place a √ for wrists still paddle-punching air
Thumbs strong, a √
but Quadratus Lumborum —
aging's howl
nags
Beginning at my toes
the tally points to *too much* and *caution*
I know.   I K<small>NOW</small>!

And all the doubt was now — will I be fit?

O—just a touch on the nape—a finger of sunlight—loving me—

Past midnight's brink
                a sunburst flashes out of sky
into everything:
                angle & cold hunch axed by light
carving boulders into high relief.
                      Mountain sprawl fires up —
clamouring now to bend its knees.

Once I was told to step up real close.
"This is a dirty dance," warned my tango tutor.
And the sun
                seductive as a Latin lover
lobs its torch
                into the virginal heart of shore-fast ice.

She wakes — her flirty eye
creamy-green up close —
                her flounced skirts permeable
as water
    in the tide-doubled pane.

Nothing clings to her
                in the shining upside-down sea
yet for me
                that fingering of sunlight on the nape —
I never want it to end.

Under the roof of the world music multiplies its songs—
seabirds pooling *kee-yah-keer-kut-a-kut-kwuk* &
narwhal misting *phweweeew* I join the mammal fray
but can't decant the undersea pitch though I'm made of water

Later the mercury skids silencing islands of ice blanching
silence skin-of-god-white and more white fracturing
the hidden moon ice doilies frazil-up the sea

God's bald pate a skating rink for birds knuckles
of rock lacing leafy rime All All inaudibly a part

Leaving Buchanan Bay for Skraeling Island again

Packing boats, I whistle between my teeth
then stagger under the hoist & carry
between shore and tide line.

Our kayaks savage the frazzle-skinned sea
carve black ribbons for passage
crewel-cutting the jewel of ice so lately brocaded.

Listen now to the ice candles toppling
like Tibetan bells they excite the brittle air
as our paddles uncouple that yeasty freeze
of fresh water's free ride on the back of brine.

*If we can inhabit an image
it must be possible to play music in it.*

—Francois Girard

EVERYTHING WAITS TO BE SEEN

We've returned to a different camp on Skraeling
islanded until wind dictates
the which-way of ice.
About a mile — it could be ten — the light letters
                            lustrous pearls
of the multi-year white menace
strung across the mouth of the fjord.

If I were a bird reconnoitering
I'd see how tide, spurring swell, could set sea-ice
packed with wind at its back:
trap us in mid-channel —
our paddles pitiful staves
against the sea-gang's swarm.

Is it not a sign of lunacy
to test my mettle with strangers?
There is risk in a place
where there are no walls
                        just sky for a roof,
where shadows have nowhere to hide.
In the populated places
the buy-me signs on every wall
compete for my eyes, but here
in the polar desert, the story
is written in bedrock (how picayune
my person alone on antediluvian shores).

The valley's slope lures me on and on
but I am not fooled, even
with time on my hands, that I
could reach the bluff in a day's hike.

I am learning to be content without my shadow,
yet still stick close to the creek's yammer
and the curly emerald mosses
soaking on wet stones.

These cool my chafing
at the delay of another day.
Look well, they implore,
so you will remember us.

As I climbed, I watched to see
how the undecided sky
massing cloud would meet the mountain top,
but it never does.

Then I turned to a dawdling day
                in Lake Joseph's childhood cottage —
recalled reading Anne of Green Gables, *vexed*
that Marilla wouldn't allow Anne-with-an-"E"
to call herself Cordelia.
                    Of course
real grief hadn't happened yet. Not until
my father died when I was ten and not knowing where to turn.

For continuing prowess I told myself
a story of strength — of that fearless Diana
who portaged a ninety-pound canoe for a quarter mile.
Her spine shivered taking the weight,
but like the Indian guides of Algonquin Park
she made the distance
                    set down the stern,
thrust up and flipped the canoe onto her knees,
slipped it to the ground, that Diana I am no more.

Once, so full of angst,
Ego   action

but silence here
redresses my mind

On the fierce edge of emptiness
a word waits

Alone in the polar desert I should know what to pray for.
The silence is so spirited.

No matter what the weather gives us, we carry on.
Living the ancient way is more than tides and tools—
the taboos I break   my iniquities stacked like carcasses
every gravel shore a killing field.
                              Here on Skraeling
seeing with eyes of the heart in this meadowed-museum
grass grows blood-lush and wind-wavy under millenial sky.
By the side of the disemboweled whale
I will pitch my tent tonight   dream the release
of beauty's beast from its magnificent cage—
its still-life trumpeting through soil.

What happened here   the great hunter
hands round the axed-off lump.
What do I know of killing   of shaman bribes,
smear of blood-blubber on my forehead.
My tame, untried hands.

I have come too late   too late
to witness the depth's great quake—
the sea giving up the perfect animal.

When sun bursts its buttons the long-dead take wing
          bones preach
 the surprised hurt of the kill
         my eye sharpens
in midnight's illumination—

a ptarmigan's spats hidden
        in willow's reach

I am lost to this wreckage of showy death
whitened off and silent among the singing flowers.
Is this not prayer   this crawling between vertebrae
holding Creation's breath between my teeth?
The sun so fat with presence.

Now I'm a Blue Bottle   a Cuckoo Bumblebee
Polaris Fritillary hooking toes into its own shadow
scale forgotten
over the fractals & fissured slopes of
                                           bones now riven
like a glacier's fist   like the
carapacious crust on a cetacean's back.

The massive arch of the behemoth's head
seems a butterfly now hinting flight
in the fluted ossifications of its white plates propped against
the instep of the Thule winter dugout,
slumped walls   a polar pack of crannies   craters
recomposing the knitting pattern
of the Mapmaker's symmetrical voice

I could lie forever in this David Milne meadow
eyes exploring cavities   those wavy
tunnels for sinew sewing together
the bowhead's radar.

Eavesdropping
              I substitute senses—
see the open roll call of the herd
the leader's voice imprinting   a bellow
a signature purr.

She thinks she's invisible on top of the rock
A gyrfalcon swooping from sky might miss her,
so wedded to the damp dun outcrop scrolled
in orange and black lichen,
too wild to be afraid,
there are no question marks in her eyes—
they see me as timid   amorphous matter
with black beak and feet   disinclined to eat
catkins and rock willow
too big to have chicks—
she clucks   clicks
lets the clockworks of her crackle
wind down to mews   soft coos—
this fearless ptarmigan
this mottled molly standing guard.

After rain, the sky
cumulates
cold rebuke
sliding down my neck
into my underpants.

I slip into my survival suit,
let yellow do the talking—
recall the Greenlandic hunter from Qaanaaq
smoking his pipe in front of the tent,
watching
my small song to nobody—
a meditation
of Qigong on bedrock.

He would be amused
at my desire to re-order
Sila's domain:
for hers is the Intelligence of the World,
the ever-changing face of weather
and dread judge of misconduct.
(How much easier it was
to tumble, on that day, into
the hills and valleys of his outstretched hand).

My bent knees take on the glacier now
and adjacent moraines,
torso reaching for sky.

I harvest all the light that's left
into my arms, believing
that roundness holds it all together.

I thought this was how to fix
the spreading of things,
but no.
No shame.
Begin again.
I bow, hands pressed.
Amen.
And still moving
as some agreeable resonance within
happens upon
the summer house of the wise *Papaver radicatum*.
Its golden face
always follows the light.

And doubt all else. But praise.

My mind muddled,
back on sensible time,
dinner at nine.
Weather plotting trouble
I feel its queer energy.

Somewhere in the Kane Basin

Light's demi-quaver flattens me
The cold, the rain —
                strategy of wait and see

From the highest point
  we glass the harbour-strew but can't
outpace Baffin's dirty sky   tracking—
the sea-ice suburbs
              poised
in a wind's minute —

                We shove off
loop through the Kane's littoral getting the litmus feel

Don't like the look of it
                Back where we started

Everything waits to be seen

Not a chair to sit on in this jury-rigged joint
   rear doors unzipped make
a longhouse for ten of us, ladder-legged,
    Inuit style, along the walls—

but silent voices of stone and bone beyond the door
whisper of spirit—remind us of
some mercy we have forgotten to ask for—
Hush   who is hunting in the violet sky?
Terns root in nests
Follow the whale—
seals at middle depth
gaze up at surly whitecaps heaving ice to shore

The wind panics   Rain lashes in
              Takes two to secure the fly
                            rocks anchoring the whipping guys

Weather hunts me   lost
to this *wayside planet's* wet and wind
                      no shorelines'
names I can put
            my finger on   to say
I am here   there
                will be

I wake
with gratitude
for the quiet
of this day
for feathered toddlers
murmuring matins
outside
my tent door.

I feel sure
after three days on Skraeling
it will be safe
to go.

the happiness in being lost in what is greater than oneself
—Teilhard de Chardin

THE WORLD MADE WHOLE

Two thirds of the voyage out   still circling away
Looping west at 76° 00' around Digarmulen Point into Hayes Fjord

I never ask how long or far the day's paddle—
                      five red kayaks snaking shore—
this steady passage
equal to the old five H.P. Johnson
powering the punt when I was a kid
                              Nothing missed

Bow-cut pries the ocean's secret white lips—
                              O   O   O
                          frothing up   sighing
                      diva's inhale   open throat—
the same dozen notes skipping rope in my mind
arms turning in a mist of paddle-drops—
                      the turning and the falling
key signatures unstable inside rhythm
as music takes flight
                            fuga spelling *rock*
The cordillera's northern measure
                1 & 2 & 3 & 4
opens the sky's one blue eye. A contrapuntal leap.

Furthermore—
my ear is tuning thirds & fifths
the igneous mind inside rock knows how to sing
and clouds dependent on wind to voice them
are finger-perfect
   —earth will not stop its extravagance
   nor grace notes alter
   the crusty planet's
   primordial cries.

The undersea crashes open
walrus shouldering fountains
A phalanx of four suck the air dry
and fork the surface
with tusk and glitter, then sink
down the sea's deep roots, whiskering for supper

In Hayes Fjord, a new camp.

I call our campsite *Ledges*
for the shoreline's smooth shoulders—
a veranda to a grand high house.

                                      Hands hugging a mug
                                      of hot tea—misting—mountains
                                      waver, grow pale.

Sky-scrim floats five kinds
of clouds—ashes of rose give way
to copper sea. We four sitting

                                        hear the machinery
                                        of lungs before we see them—
                                        walrus, pulsing air.

Mid-fjord, an island
like potter's clay in the palm,
forgotten by God.

I was ten when I bruised my thigh
rubber booting the Madawaska   falling
into a rainy-day river tumbling into my ears

keeping track — rivering up meanders
years   hardly matters which   this falling up   into

the nearest approach to an Arctic paradise
            — George Strong Nares, 1875

(shore boulders also plum-bruised when wet)

Now   I top Ledges' high meadow   traversing
the tall cliff's haunch   coupled

to unsung gardens of blue stars
soil's spongy peat-pack   moss-lime
loving sun   opening for it

                                it could be
evensong side-slipping the scent of ice   earth's
damp languor loving my cheek

uneasiness plumb forgotten   I stoop
to braided streams

don't fence me in
direction losing its way   looking for solid ground
                                 the long way round

                                   I overshoot the descent

Just once, I'd like to see the way
the great grey ice-flats of the Lincoln Sea
begin their southward haul. How
the melting sheets   shear
then choke the channel that feeds the fjords.

I can hear
the wrath of seven-storied ice,
its teeth and steel   castling
& cantilevering rafts.

The map declares its own stories of despair—
Thank God Havn no haven
to the man who ate his boots—
hear his twelve-tone crescendo.
See how his hands trembled.

By now, the yearly outflow is
harbouring in Hayes and Buchanan Bay
where tide's little finger lifts the summer's catch
from the Polar hub,
litters the shores.

And me not noticing
                how rain can loosen a floater's grip on rock
'til twenty feet from my bow
           shore ice plummets

                The ocean gulps a season
reminding me what brute force is in it
                and I feel
winter's revenge on summer in the waves' attack

                Back up, orders Scott
don't want that ice coming up under us

In my imagination
the ice-stump big as a house
(but really shed-sized, or mudroom more)
impregnates the bed of the sea—
Scott & I concussed
inside the belt of the foaming funnel,
tonnage at our backs.
What cold feels like and fading.

   I looked upon the rim's revolutions,
   the swaying seam and boil—
   the flotsam's precipitous descent.

What I do not recall,
the vortex vomiting the meal—
that white beauty up-rise into sight again—
or obedient to gravity, diving yet—
either way, that close call a sub-zero note.
I do not know why we never spoke of it.
We never did.

But really, what was there to say—
Have I been handed back my life again
although it was not taken?
For there was an imperfect death
imperfectly understood.
A threshold, as I learn I have to learn
again and again, how the universe recreates itself.
I feel its order even as
the ice-stump sheers from rock,
violates the sea-smooth sea
and instantly begins to melt, replacing timeless
evaporation.

Circadian coherence says
I am part of organic necessity—
my time is coming, but not yet.

I notice how we never raise our voices
never shout—
some constraint of courtesy perhaps
imposed by the hieratic silence.

Meanwhile, I say this to myself,
tremendum dei a way to comprehend my place—
a homage

*The pond on top of Outer Island is overflowing,
our proposed new camp under water. Drizzle pits
the windless ocean. We return to Ledges.
Over hot pasta, sudden bonechill
rears the hairs on my neck.*

Marty, Chris & Gerry
sail my half-rigged tent
to a gravel elevation,
peg me down, tie me in.

I go to ground in my down bag,
curl up like a stone.
I am ready, Oh Lord of the Winds.
Navigate me through this night,
show me once again
that here is now.
This moment.
That hearing is listening.

*I do not wish to affirm what I already know.
I do not mind when we return.*
                                          Talk to me.

And a wind, like Jeremiah on a rampage, slams the walls, screaming,
Repent! Repent! R   !   R   !
           My tent, quick to appease, lest he hurl
thunderbolts too, bends its knees to the heave of floor. I am
the weight that holds a paper to the ground. See how helpless I am
against this Old Testament voice, emptying sky's width of air.

Again, I wait for the wind's big stick,
exhilarated now when it hurls
its dry waves at my door.
Then suddenly it stops —
I drop from a great height inside myself
and know for a fact my fear of leaving here,
the throaty silence I have come to —
how it calls to me like a pent-up sea.
This is what I had waited for.
That voice inside the wind's shadow.

Here — no separation
A world made whole.

NOTES

STILLNESS HAS AN ECHO
Skraeling: the origin of the word is disputed but Old Norse legend suggests the name comes from "skin-cloth," referring to the indigenous people who dressed in skins, and were encountered by the Norse from the 11th Century onward. Another interpretation, working backward from today's Scandinavian languages, offers "weaklings" as a descriptive of the people. Explorer Otto Sverdrup renamed the island Skraeling in 1898, from the original Three Sisters, so called by George Nares.

Sedna was the vengeful spirit who made her abode at the bottom of the sea. When a taboo was broken, she took all the sea animals into her house and hid them. Then the starving humans would send the shaman to visit her, and by combing out the lice in her hair persuaded her to release the animals again.

HOW BIG IS THE WORLD
Maktaaq is the edible skin and blubber layers of the narwhal.

Riphean refers to the stage in the geological timescale of Earth, denoting a period about a 1000 million years ago.

Life would not yield to age, Edgar's Lament, *King Lear* Act IV, Sc. 1.

I HAVE WORSHIPPED LIGHT
Connell epigraph from *Notes from a Bottle Found on the Beach at Carmel.*

And all the doubt was now — should I be fit? "Childe Roland," VII, Robert Browning.

EVERYTHING WAITS TO BE SEEN
Francois Girard, quoted from CD notes, *The Cello Suites: Yo-Yo Ma.*

Sila is one of many powerful spirits which ruled human life. She represented both weather and consciousness, and it was under the threat of her punishment that the humans adhered to the taboos and rituals that ensured survival.

And doubt all else. But praise, from John Ciardi, "The Heron."

THE WORLD MADE WHOLE
George Strong Nares was a British naval officer and Arctic explorer, who sailed on the *Resolute* in search of the Sir John Franklin expedition of 1852–54. He was the first white man to see Skraeling Island in 1875.

ACKNOWLEDGEMENTS

My thanks to Don McKay, Stan Dragland and Marilyn Bowering for their unfailing encouragement while I was attending the 2005 Banff Writing Studio and for getting me started on this book.

For continuing help and friendship from Allan Briesmaster, gratitude.

Heartfelt thanks to Signature Editions and George Payerle, editor, whose astute ear and eye continually amaze me. Namaste.

To Phil Hall, my good friend and accomplice, for tinkering & tilting & listening, special thanks.

For fine-tuning on some poems by Sue Chenette, Donna Langevin, Katie Marshall Flaherty, Chris Pannell — my appreciation.

Many thanks to John MacDonald from Nunavut for sharing his knowledge of Inuktitut.

Earlier versions of some poems incorporated here appeared in the following publications: *Queen's Quarterly, Talk That Mountain Down* (Littlefishcartpress), and *The Saving Bannister, 25th Anthology.*

To "Whitney and Smith" who provided the means, my gratitude.

Kudos to my paddling partners: Denise and Scott, our trusty guides; Cookie and Gerry from Alberta; Dale, Brand, Chris and Marty from the USA, and Luciano Napolitano from Italy.

Stormy Weather is a song by Cole Porter.

ABOUT THE AUTHOR

Rosemary Clewes was born in Toronto and enjoyed several careers, as a script assistant for CBC television, a social worker, then printmaker and now writer/poet.

Over the last decade, her poems have been published in many literary journals. She was nominated by *The Malahat Review* for The National Magazine Awards in 2005, and a year later was a finalist for the CBC Literary Awards.

Her first book of prose and poetry, *Thule Explorer: Kayaking North of 77 Degrees* (Hidden Brook Press) was published in 2008 and remains a fine primer for Arctic adventurers.

Clewes has travelled many times to the Arctic by kayak, raft and icebreaker.

ECO-AUDIT
*Printing this book using Rolland Opaque50
instead of virgin fibres paper saved the following resources:*

Trees	Solid Waste	Water	Air Emissions
1	70 kg	3,013 L	218 kg